# Shining Mead

The Author as an Aristocrat of the Soul

# Shining Mead

Poems Inspired by
Life, Conjunction, and Occultism

Eirik Westcoat

Skaldic Eagle Press
Long Branch, Pennsylvania
2025

Copyright © 2025 Eirik Westcoat
All rights reserved.

For permissions or other information, please contact the author at <eirik@theskaldiceagle.com> or <www.theskaldiceagle.com>.

Cover photo by Albo Greene
All layout and design by Eirik Westcoat

First Edition, Winter Nights 2025

9 8 7 6 5 4 3 2

Black & White Trade Paperback
ISBN: 978-1-947407-16-9

Skaldic Eagle Press
Long Branch, Pennsylvania

*For Tradition*

# Acknowledgments

Thanks go to Herne Siegmann and others unnamed for comments on the poems prior to publication. I especially thank all of the women referred to in these poems, both human (whether lovers or not) and supernatural. Thanks go also to my blog and Patreon subscribers who saw drafts of many of these poems in advance. And special thanks go to Albo Greene for the cover photo, which is of the Great American Total Solar Eclipse of August 21, 2017. You can find Albo's work at <albofilm.com>.

Some text and image and credits are needful here:
- The poem "The Emerald Tablet" is my verse rendering of the classic hermetic text. In creating it, I consulted the many available translations at <sacred-texts.com/alc/emerald.htm>.
- The 1618 print "The Invisible College of the Rose Cross Fraternity" by Theophilus Schweighardt from *Speculum Sophicum Rhodo-Stauroticum* is in the public domain.
- In the Háskólavísur 2014–2016 chapter, I took both of the photos there and retain the copyright to them.
- The Wewelsburg sun wheel image used at the end of the text is my remixed version (by adding a core to the center of the design) of the one by the user Blacksonne on this page: <commons.wikimedia.org/wiki/File:The_Black_Sun.svg>.
It is available via a Creative Commons license, CC BY-SA 4.0, <creativecommons.org/licenses/by-sa/4.0/>, copyright 2016. My remixed version is released under the same license and available in digital format at <www.theskaldiceagle.com>. I call this symbol the Round Table Sun Wheel.

Several poems here are inspired by essays in my companion book to this one, *Occult Mead: Essays on Runes, Grails, and the Round Table Sun Wheel*. Mostly, these are the poems on Triadic Experiences, Eagle and Gar, Moldavite, and the Round Table Sun Wheel. I encourage my readers here to obtain that volume as well.

Lastly, this book would not be possible without the three guiding stars of my Work: Óðrœrir, Rûna, and the Grail.

# Table of Contents

Preface ............................................................................. x

*Mission*

Poetic Revolution ............................................................. 2
A Skaldic Eagle Takes Flight ............................................. 4
A Skaldic Eagle in the World ............................................ 6
A Skaldic Manifesto ......................................................... 8
Tradition and Modernity ................................................ 10

*Trees*

Black Walnut .................................................................. 14
The Yew .......................................................................... 16
Hanging from a Tree ...................................................... 18
The Roots of Trees .......................................................... 20
The Flow of Nine Worlds ............................................... 22
Eagle and Gar ................................................................. 24

*Observational*

What is Absinthe? ........................................................... 26
Identification .................................................................. 28
Pilgrimage ....................................................................... 30
Sometimes a Cigar Is Just a Poem .................................. 32
Xicoy and the Heart ....................................................... 34
Volcano ........................................................................... 36
Snowfall across the Worlds ............................................. 38

*Political*

Against Polarization and Hate ........................................ 40
I'm with Them ................................................................ 43
Make Yourself Great Again ............................................ 44
Ancient and Modern Dragons ....................................... 46
The Conflict .................................................................... 48

*Alliterative Sonnets*

    Fire and Ice .................................................................. 50
    A Hanged Man ............................................................ 51
    Iceland as Thule ........................................................... 52
    Industry and Sloth ....................................................... 53
    The Odian Wanderer .................................................. 54

*Esotericism*

    Moldavite: Stone and Grail .......................................... 56
    The Emerald Tablet ..................................................... 59
    Total Solar Eclipse ....................................................... 60
    Triadic Experiences ..................................................... 63
    Sonnenrad or So-Called "Black Sun" ........................... 64
    Round Table Sun Wheel ............................................. 68
    Et in Arcadia Ego ........................................................ 70
    Hyperborea: The Polar Seat ......................................... 72
    Call to the "Rosicrucians" ............................................ 74

*Personal*

    The Black Dog ............................................................ 78
    Beautiful Darknesses ................................................... 81
    Fertility ........................................................................ 85
    Farewell ....................................................................... 87
    Luciidrápa ................................................................... 88
    Tide ............................................................................. 92
    Ærdna ......................................................................... 94
    Fire, Ashes, and Rebirth .............................................. 96

*Háskólavísur 2014–2016*

    01: Infamous Foods .................................................. 100
    02: The Winds of Reykjavík ..................................... 101
    03: My Heathen Hof ................................................. 102
    04: Imagine Peace Tower ........................................... 103
    05: First Snow in Reykjavík ...................................... 104

06: The Battles of Sæmundargata .................................................105
07: Nýtt Ár Ríma ..........................................................................106
08: Climb the Mountain ..............................................................107
09: The Heart of the Slain ...........................................................108
10: The Suns of Summer .............................................................109
11: Nýtt Land og Nýja Hof ..........................................................110
12: The Semester Sets In .............................................................111
13: The Turning Wheel ...............................................................112
14: The End of the Degree ..........................................................114
15: Saga's End .............................................................................116

*Invocations*

Xicoy Invocation ........................................................................120
Theobroma Invocation ..............................................................121
Cigar Invocation ........................................................................122
Cigarillo Invocation ...................................................................123
Cannabis Invocation ..................................................................124
Hrapé Invocation .......................................................................125
Coffee Invocation .......................................................................126
Water Invocation .......................................................................127
Call to the Green Fairy ...............................................................128
Moldavite Invocation .................................................................129
Solar Glory Invocation ...............................................................130
Runic Sun Invocation .................................................................131
Round Table Sun Wheel Invocation ...........................................132

# Preface

This is my first new poetry collection in over six years. And it is another new kind of book for me, not a repeat of or a sequel to one of its predecessors. My first poetry book, *Viking Poetry for Heathen Rites*, was a collection of ritual poetry and other predominantly heathen religious and mythological verse. My second poetry book, *Eagle's Mead*, was a collection of runic, heathen magical, and occult verse, with a few essays. These two earlier poetry books were grand gestures of a size and scope that may have intimidated some—but which those books insisted upon. However, this book, which you are currently reading, insisted on something different. It wanted to be an "ordinary" poetry book, and it is in many ways, but yet it is nonetheless far from ordinary in other ways.

It is ordinary in that most of the poems here are much more personal than in my earlier books. And I travel beyond the confines of strictly Heathen and Asatru topics to broader fields of spirituality, occultism, and everyday life. But the book is beyond ordinary through the perspectives I bring and the ways in which I write: an orientation toward the spiritual, the transcendent, and the realm of Tradition where the gods live, along with the steadfast use of traditional alliterative verse throughout. The main verse form in this book is what I call "Anglo-Saxon continuous verse," which is more or less the style found in *Beowulf*, for instance. A few poems add rhymes to this (the alliterative sonnets), and a few others use Norse or Icelandic forms. And so they are literary poems, but of an extraordinary, instead of ordinary, sort. (But see my poem "A Skaldic Manifesto" for how I've positioned myself vis-à-vis the MFA and Slam Poetry scenes.)

Though I am not inclined to be trendy with so-called "trigger warnings," I still respect the old-school warnings of the movie- and-television rating kind regarding content appropriate for children. So you should beware that some of these poems contain politics, Nazi occultism, tobacco, cannabis, or explicit sexual content—material that is not suitable for young children. Consider yourself warned. But that is only a few of the poems.

Most of the poems here were written from 2017 to 2021, during the time I was preparing for or in a PhD program in Iceland. But some of them are from either before or after that period. And regardless of time period, they are informed by the occult and esoteric perspectives I've acquired through my work in the Rune-Gild and the once-and-future Guild of the Grail. But I won't go into detail about those schools or perspectives here. The interested reader may see more direct manifestations of my work in those schools in my earlier book *Eagle's Mead* and my companion book to this one, *Occult Mead*. Now for some remarks on the individual chapters to orient the reader:

- "Mission" contains poems about my poetry, my being a poet, and the bold mission of my poetry in the world.

- "Trees" contains poems about my two favorite trees, the black walnut and the yew, and other poems about the symbolism of trees, especially from a Norse mythological perspective.

- "Observational" contains my poetic commentaries on several topics and experiences of a general nature.

- "Alliterative Sonnets" contains my first several poems in a new form which is based on the rhyming Shakespearean sonnet, but is changed to use alliterative lines instead of iambic pentameter, and to variously use 9, 18, or 27 lines total instead of 14.

- "Esotericism" contains the most occult poems of this book (that is, the ones whose topics are overtly so), including one of the last in this book to be written, "Round Table Sun Wheel." It is my poem about the real identity (which had long been a mystery) of the infamous sun wheel design in Wewelsburg Castle. My companion book to this one, *Occult Mead: Essays on Runes, Grails, and the Round Table Sun Wheel*, contains my essay, "Wewelsburg's So-Called 'Black Sun' Is Really Himmler's Round Table and Grail," in which I make my case for that identity. My poem "Total Solar Eclipse" is about my experience of the eclipse of August 21, 2017.

- "Personal" contains poems on the most personal topics I've ever written about. Here, there are poems about depression, serious injury, romance, girlfriends, and sex. At least one of these is rather explicit. You have been warned.

- "Háskólavísur 2014–2016" contains most of the oldest poems in this book. It is a series of short poems usually accompanied by a bit of prose (the technical term is prosimetrum) in which I wrote about various experiences during my two years in the Viking and Medieval Norse Studies MA/MPhil program at the Universities of Iceland and Oslo. The narrative tone of this chapter is meant to be an adaptation of saga style.

- "Invocations" is the final chapter and contains poems the reader might even try reciting out loud to invoke the spirits and beings mentioned. A number of them relate back to poems in the preceding chapters. This is the chapter with most of the tobacco and cannabis references, as may be surmised from the titles. It closes with an invocation to the Round Table Sun Wheel.

Finally, this is a book for those who hope to see a literary revival of traditional verse. It is poetry qua poetry in proper alliterative meters without apology or pretentiousness. It is poetry expressing a spiritual vision oriented toward Transcendence that's synthesized with Seeking the Mysteries. And though this book is quite different from *Eagle's Mead*, it is nevertheless also a book for initiates, magicians, occultists, esotericists, sages, heathen prophets, and other travelers of the hidden realms. May they enjoy these signposts to Spirit.

Eirik Westcoat  
Winter Nights 2025

# Mission

## Poetic Revolution

You say you want serious revolution?
To rework the world? 'Tisn't why I'm here!
Why? What is it? Well, listen now,
it's the past's power for poetry today.
This heathen writer, from reading history,
brings to his verse the Viking meters,
filled with old lore, formerly ancient,
made fresh today for folk of the now.
So what? Why now? Well, it's because. . .
this modern world is a mountain of sand!
So I strive instead to stand my poems
on the granite bedrock of greatest myths,
leaving behind lesser matter.
How is it done? Here I will say.
From truths of old, make trends anew.
With tales of heroes, train your spirit,
for poetry is the power of mead:
that awesome brew that Óðinn stole
from jealous giants who enjoyed it not.
It's seeking inside the secret runes,
in spirit whispers speaking within.
It's lighting the dark that lurks in the mind,
in corners covered by cobwebs thick.
It's pressing hard the past tradition
in books of lore for a bounty of juice.
Take that pressing and pitch in yeast;
own that ferment and age it well.
Savor that wine as a soul-tonic

to change yourself for changing the world.
Work for Ascent, seeking to rise
to the heights among the high mountains,
electing yourself to the elite of spirit.
Then share that spark and shine with others
to light the lives that live in darkness.
Such aristocrats of the soul will speak new runes
into this crapped-up world of the Kali Yuga.
Thus they will strive and then at last
reworking the world may well just happen.
This likely isn't the revolution you sought,
but for better or worse, it's the one I'm bringing:
a return to tradition from the tired postmodern
with time-tested truths o'er transient fads.

# A Skaldic Eagle Takes Flight

Hatched from the Egg, he was hungry always;
that cosmic hailstone crafted such wyrd.
In size he surged, consuming carrion:
strong and stately, he stood at last.
He was sleek and fierce, but unsatisfied.
That fleshy fodder had fulfilled its end,
but such food no longer could feed his soul.
His keen cold eyes, they craved new vistas,
and his heart sought out the holy mysteries.
To the Cave he went, that court of darkness
and Lunar land of limitless night,
seeking its treasures for his soul's triumph.
He came at last to cauldrons three
filled with the ferment of fathomless Spirit.
He drank down that Mead and from dreams awoke
to soul's satisfaction and Solar gnosis.
A seed of Self he saw within,
and now at last he knew himself
as the eagle he was. Then up he flew;
to the heights he soared and their healthful freedom;
the sun he sought in Ascent and joy.
With gnosis now of these new vistas,
he poured out poetry in a powerful torrent,
a sparkling stream of Spirit's essence.
He remembered the land and meant to return,
but gray and grim the ground realms seemed;
one tear he shed for that world he'd lost,
though aid he'd offer to the others down there

by decanting Mead to the curious ones
who sought the Sky. Ere soaring again
(above-aiming to the abode of Spirit),
on the taller trees for a time he'd rest,
and among the majesty of the mountain peaks.
Truly this happens, time and again:
the birth and rebirth—a bittersweet tale—
of a Skaldic Eagle in the Sky above.

# A Skaldic Eagle in the World

A Skaldic Eagle must offer his Mead,
must give his gifts, for gain to the World;
the Work is imperative, a wode-filled impulse.
But defending the Center 'gainst foes and shadows
—that its sacred light illumines unimpeded
a world of darkness—is a woesome task.
And even an eagle must often land,
and life on the ground can get one down,
with its oft-assaulting slings and arrows.
To endure the squalls, a Skaldic Eagle
must stay a course that's steady and true,
with might and main on a Middle Path,
not eschewing extremes but choosing both,
and with an inner core that's anchored in Spirit,
synthesize both into Sacred Mead—
'tis the eternal task of all true Masters.
What's this Eagle's task, his toilsome journey?
To offer enlightenment to all true seekers,
with open dialogue and the awesome Runes,
which belong to all who lift them up
—full stop, forsooth—from the fimbul darkness.
To inspire others to spiritual purpose
and a higher life to enhance their growth
with the brimming Mead, for by bread alone,
one cannot live, one cannot thrive.
Each finds The Good in the forms and idioms
that are suited to oneself and can seek from there
collective grounds for life in the world,

to be for something, in fullest truth,
not fashionably "against" in affected grandstanding.
What's this Eagle's way, his Work that effects?
Mandatory are my quests: for Mead, Runes, and Grails.
Small-minded people will oppress and assail me.
So far, some have: too seriously they take
themselves in their strikes. By standing for something,
one will get enemies; it's an inevitable fact.
When showing one's light in shining brilliance,
the dwellers in darkness will deem it offense.
But I'm called nonetheless, and must carry on,
to muster courage for that Middle Path
and to rebuke the bigots of both extremes.
Over it all, my "identity" as such
comes forth from craft and vocations' paths.
Do good I must to good people,
for doom is deemed by deeds o'er all,
not belief, not identity. Look, here's the truth:
the quests are my guide; the quests are my light.
Not pompous nor political, they are personal, spiritual.
Inspiration irrupts, and I render my Mead.
The Mysteries exist, and with zeal I seek them.
The Mountain beckons, and I make my way up.
Mead, Runes, and Grails: the mighty whole
is contained in those three, truly it is,
and the rest is commentary, though a rightful guide.
Thus goes the path of this Glory Eagle.

# A Skaldic Manifesto

A "Diss"—at first, this dignified verse
was planning to be a poem like that.
But it's not my style, though *níð* has its place.
'Tis better here to broadcast my mission,
to say what I'm *for*, than to slam what I'm against.
You can try it then, to determine what are
the various things I'm in revolt against.
The modern world, Midgard today,
is where I must land and work my magic
through the verse I write; I'll venture an account.
In what school of poetry is the Skaldic Eagle?
I'm a brand-new bird, born of old roots.
I write Viking poetry, in Viking meters,
to bring the Old Gods and the boons of their ways
to today's Midgard. It definitely needs them.
I craft my words to proclaim the ways
of Óðinn to Man. I'm an archeo-formalist
who exalts Spirit in a zany world.
New Formalism was a needed start,
but it doesn't dare to do what's needed.
They dusted off the ancient skeleton
and stood it up, but that's still not enough.
The ancient bones won't reanimate
in that sterile way, stillborn they'd be.
Alchemy is needed, that noble Art,
for going further and galdoring truly
to join them all in judicious measure:
first bone to bone as the best foundation,

then sinew to sinew, safely together,
then flesh to flesh for fimbul strength,
then blood to blood for brightest vigor,
and skin to skin with skillful Art.
Slam has spirit, but Spirit it lacks
in its secular mire, with the sacred missing.
MFA has craft, but its art is rigid
in an academic manner, and also secular.
None of the three could nourish my soul
when they muck in the dark of dreary materialism,
not seeking the Mead, the Mysteries, or Ascent.
I'm of an age when the origin of poetry
was with the gods as a wode-filled art,
a mighty Mead made from a god,
and its sacred power surged through the world
in mighty words that worked magic,
making things happen for Midgard's people.
A poetry that's part and parcel of the sacred.
While others work in a world that's mundane,
always I must go with the avant-garde
of Traditionalism in poetry, a daring quest,
and build new temples on the truest bedrock,
creating a space where Spirit may dwell
and the Gods be summoned to gift our world
in the verse that once gave vigor to them,
restoring wholeness to a stilted world
and relinking Man to relation with the Sacred.

# Tradition and Modernity

A World of Tradition, A World of Modernity:
the one was lost in the waxing of the other.
But dire is the doom that Modernity has wrought:
our Western World is at war with itself.
Conflict is everywhere, a fight that's existential,
and ruled by capital, we're really in a fix.
Whence did it come? What can we do?
Great gains we've made, growing in power,
with methods and machines to manifest will
in a Faustian bid for a future unlimited.
But we lost our souls—those lights within—
and technology's gains have had a noxious price:
they are terrible masters that've taken as slaves
the societies they should serve, setting the people
as servants instead. And the servants fight,
squabbling bitterly with squalor abounding,
with the people treating the people as things,
as if *they* were the machines—*this* must be stopped.
Our hearts cry out for a higher life.
Recovering our souls is the call we've to answer,
to bring new meaning back to our lives.
Since no powerful zealotry can dissolve the people
and elect a new one (though the louts have tried),
we must live in this world and bring light to it,
peacefully together or peacefully separate.
Tradition is the way, which deemed an order
of family, community, and fulfilling tribes,
with religious life as a link to the Sacred,

so that all had meaning to orient their lives
and see a world—a serious one—
that's filled with subjects (not simple objects)
to accept and honor for the souls they have.
That would bring healing—a balm much needed—
first and foremost to our fellows and ourselves
and then to living biomes in land, air, and water.
But can we get there and keep the gains
—for working our will—of the world today?
A World of Tradition, A World of Modernity:
is synthesis possible? Synthesize we must,
to bridge the impasse, break the stasis,
and stand anew in a stable Center,
where we are ordered inside and ordered outside.
Where will it start? In one place truly.
Synthesis begins inside our hearts,
for each in their own, and only then
can the Work go out to a World that needs it.

# Trees

# Black Walnut

A mighty tree, an American treasure,
is *Juglans nigra*, the Union's walnut.
Warm, humid air with welcome sunshine
favors its growth in a fine summer.
'Tis green everywhere: green are the leaves,
green the flowers, and green the fruits.
The inside is sealed by a silver-gray bark;
placed underneath, with a pungent scent,
is a staining substance—a strong essence—
that yellows and browns in the yawning air.
The whitest of woods is the way for its sap,
with a splendid grain, especially nice,
and concealing inside a center of richness,
a heart of darkness, highly valued
for consummate crafts. Coveted also
is its peerless nut, prized for its flavor
far well beyond the walnut varieties
in the world elsewhere. You'll work for a taste:
intensely hard, it's tough to crack
—you'll need a vise, a nutcracker
of the kitchen kind just can't prevail—
but ambrosia awaits, buried within.
Some would yet scoff and say it's a weed,
the way it springs up and waxes with nuts,
an early pioneer in open spaces,
seeking always the sun in full.
If only weeds were all like this!
But what is its essence, its inner nature?

With noble bearing, the Black Walnut,
in heart and nut, is highly Solar:
bright sun outside makes black sun inside
and a rich sweet taste in the regal core
of its modest fruit. With mighty roots
and sturdy hard wood for standing upright,
its elegant limbs aim for the sky
as a true aristocrat among righteous trees.
So ponder this beam, and appreciate better
the sun above through this sun on the ground.

# The Yew

The Tree of Trees for triumph I praise,
that fimbul rood and focus of Spirit,
a gift of the Gods for the gain of Midgard.
A lustrous light, it is life in death
when the coldest snow surrounds our ken.
For the noble Norse and numerous others,
it is majesty, main, and myth-saturated;
for the steadfast English, 'tis the estate's joy.
Hail to the Yew, holy and ancient—
for serious seekers, a most sorcerous wood.
'Tis fire's keeper and a force of nature,
with deep green needles—it dreams of eternity
as the world's witness, watching through centuries—
and orange-brown heart, awesome in might,
and bright red berries, a boon in the fall
and blessing of sweetness, yet bearing poison
in the kernel within, a clash of opposites.
The gallows of the god who gained the runes,
its heavy presence hinders evil,
its limbs live after as luck-filled tines,
and its eternal spirit teems with those runes,
even as itself is an awesome Rune.
It goes slow in growth, seeking good skies;
even as a shrub, it shines with magic.
Yet once it's large, it waxes in might,
an intense, overpowering titanic essence.
'Tis a small part come of the Superworld
and set in the ordinary as a sign that points

to the inviolable Center, to the invisible Pole.
Identified with Yggdrasil, what *does* this mean?
The nine bright words this needle ash bears,
from Hel below in lands of darkness
to Asgard above in awesome splendor.
And you yourself, like the Yews on earth
contain these worlds in your total being,
as well as its wights—a wondrous zoo—
the eagle, the serpent, and all the rest.
So hang in spirit on this holy tree
and make yourself into this mainful beam—
or rather, realize that this rood is within
to gain its mysteries, the greater and lesser,
to make it a joy on your mortal estate.
As the olden bow of archers past,
it sent forth their arrows to find their targets;
send forth your will with its fimbul staves.
Work with its wood, gain wode with it,
for the mightiest magics of majesty and growth,
for poetry's power, and plenty else—
just look within and journey deeply
into the Sacred Heart of the holy Yew.

# Hanging from a Tree

That's how he did it, by hanging from a tree,
how Óðinn won the ancient runes.
He challenges us to change our lives
by seeking those mysteries. And so we must,
by hanging also on a hallowed tree.
But what is Yggdrasil, and where might it be,
that we may ride that rood for its runic treasures?
Everywhere, throughout and in all of the world,
the trunk, the roots, and the towering branches
of that runic tree are running, everywhere.
But gods we are not, so go for a tree
that's a tiny part of the total whole.
For each who has eyes, they're all around:
literal and figurative, both large and small.
Person by person, those pines will vary,
so seek a tree for your singular truth.
A regular tree at the Ramblewood site
isn't often special, but the Spirit emerged
when, with hooks in my back that harrowing night,
an ordinary tree was Yggdrasil for me,
stretching my skin and stretching my mind.
With time enough, I obtained the runes,
through toil after. Toil? Yes, indeed,
for work we must, for that wondrous gain.
For a limited being, laying infinity
into the soul and body is a serious task
that is wholly analogous to another hanging.
If nights all nine were needed by Óðinn,

then longer, surely, for a living man,
is the work of winning that wondrous gain!

## The Roots of Trees

Consider a tree, seemingly ordinary,
to learn the model and life of the others:
the tree within and the Tree without.
Of trees we see the trunk and branches
with beautiful leaves and bright flowers:
luscious wonders. But lurking beneath
the soil's surface are the secret roots
in that darkest realm of deep unknowns,
where mysteries lurk, tremendous Runes.
So, to truly know a tree's full life,
look to those roots and what lurks among them.
Look to your tree, and learn your mysteries.
Look to the Tree, and learn its Mysteries.
This initiation of needful growth
begins in darkness but goes to the light.
What will you find in your wondrous tree?
What will you find in the wondrous Tree?
Travel the trunk and take to the roots
for the worlds below and the wells with orlog.
Traditions slumber and dreams await,
deep in those roots. Dare to raise them,
lift what reposes from the Land of the Dead.
Find What was Lost, for its fimbul might
brings life anew to leaf and flower
on a tree that's troubled and triumph aplenty
to a tree that's strong. The truest of changes
are wrought with the boons from that realm below

which lead to the realm of light above,
the crown in the heights with its clear pure view.

# The Flow of Nine Worlds

All was Yggdrasil to the ancient Norse,
a fathomless Tree that framed the worlds,
nine in number, into a united whole.
Ginnungagap, a great emptiness,
was there in the beginning and there alone.
Still it'd have stayed, but there started a flow,
the first of flows, which formed the worlds.
Ice upwelling from the outer North
met fire flaming from the farthest South,
and a hailstone was made in the heart of it all,
Ymir at first, and Auðumbla then.
The eldest Gods and etins were formed
as the flow continued, finding new paths.
But Sigföður knew that something was lacking,
that greater worlds were going unmade,
so Ymir he slew, reordering his parts
into that awesome Tree that is Yggdrasil now.
Nine are the worlds it nurtures and grows,
keeping them balanced by careful design:
the worlds and their flows must work together.
'Twixt Nifl' and Muspell', the numbing ice
and flaming fire does flow yet still.
'Twixt Vana' and Jötun' are the vital energies
of growth and resistance for glorious life.
'Twixt Asgard and Hel, highest and lowest,
are action and stillness for alternating motion.
'Twixt Svartálf' and Ljósálf', below and above,
are shaping and intention for shepherding will.

But here in Midgard, in the middle of all flow,
we live, we die, we learn, and we grow.
For boom or bust, the balance is ours,
to maintain and manage in this middle world,
or to carelessly wreck and cause destruction.
But now it seems that Nature is threatened
by the insensitive abuse of our central position,
by behaving as if humans are gods
and high above the whole of existence.
So needed dearly is a renewal of wisdom
to fix the flows that bring fates of ill.
But the outside realms are only a part
of the whole picture; the whole of those flows
is also within, for the elder poets
kenned us as trees, since crafty Óðinn
made people as well from primal trees.
Our inner flows are also critical,
and we are bound to try to balance them too.
Balance within and balance without
for the flows within and the flows without:
to heal ourselves and heal the world,
our course must be this, it cannot be else.

# Eagle and Gar

I hail the Eagle as I hang on the Tree
for nights all nine of Needful Work.
Wounded by Gar, I give my self
to my higher Self in holy sacrifice.
The Eagle glares with greedy eyes,
ready to feed on the runes of my flesh.
The wind whistles, the wood shakes hard,
my ego dies, and the Eagle feasts.
A new "I" awakes with the noble Runes,
screaming fiercely and surging with Wode.
And now I know that I was never a self,
but always the Eagle that has eaten me.
And gladly I know that the Gar I wield
for works in the world is the wood of my being,
the ritual weapon that wounded me,
and the windy Tree, all one in the same,
forged from the Runes that I realized truly.

# Observational

# What is Absinthe?

What is absinthe? An emerald aperitif?
A wormwood wine? A welcome muse?
'Tis all of these and also more.
It is Wormwood grand, a wizard of herbs,
and awesome Anise of excellent spirit,
and far-famed Fennel, a fortunate plant,
with other herbs—absinthe is this.
The proof is high in this potent brew,
but much more beyond is this mighty liquor.
To artists of old and honored poets,
'twas a graceful angel of glorious inspiration,
a goddess of awe: the Green Fairy!
Picasso and Crowley had called to her;
Dowson and Degas were drinkers as well.
Though long her absence, absinthe's returned!
You can't keep her down, this crafty lady.
But is she alone, or allied this time?
What muses move with this mighty lass?
A few perhaps from famed Old Greece?
Or is it Óðrœrir, the awesome mead,
that tries this time to return to the world.
Seek and explore her spirit yourself.
Try and test her. Truly it's easy.
Pour some absinthe in an artful glass;
Then set a spoon with sucrose on top.
Carefully decant some cold ice water,
releasing the louche in this liquid poem.
Dazzling your eyes, the drink will change

from a clear emerald to a cloudy opal.
Such right ritual readies her gifts.
Approach with respect and proffer invocations
to welcome her spirit. Well remember
that always best is to offer yourself,
giving your ghost to her green embrace.
Then drink it deeply, this draught of poets;
like at mass commune with the muse's spirit.
Clarity you'll gain from her cloudy drink,
and maybe a glimpse of mysteries hidden,
as a sage once said, to see what's wished,
to see what's not, and to see what's real.
In composing this poem, I poured her spirit,
drinking and draining draughts aplenty,
for knowing her well was needful deeply.
From that I say this simple advice:
seek the substance o'er the simple accidents,
and you just might find that joyful goddess:
the Green Fairy of glorious absinthe.

## Identification

What are you, really? The walking rudiments
of upward evolution to an Übermensch?
If you'd aim for that goal of ultimate Ascent,
sorting yourself is seriously needful,
to know what you're not and know what you are.
Runes aplenty are realized in the process.
You have a body, but here's the truth,
you're not your body—you need to experience
this fact intensely as a feeling in your bones
to further your growth. Fit you should keep it,
but it's just not you. Judge next your emotions,
those fluid phantoms of fleeting sensations.
Tougher this is, they're a tangled mess
not firmly grasped 'twixt finger and thumb:
they're hard to locate, whether hate or love
or anger or others. Always remember,
your "I" has emotions, but emotions you aren't.
You have a mind—a Huginn and Muninn,
both thought and memory—but think carefully,
for you are not your mind, though needful it is.
It often refuses to answer to you!
What about wode, the wonder of inspiration?
You're not that either, but now you can
better contemplate its being and role,
a crucial force for the clever skald
and for working magic. What could be left,
after all of that? Only your center
of will and self, the one who sees,

the ultimate subject of the objects you have:
your mutable mind, emotions, and body.
With that diamond spark, identify yourself
for the upward evolution of your inner being.

# Pilgrimage

My great pilgrimage gains momentum
in a Honda Civic on a highway turnpike
through a lengthy drive to the land of Michigan
with a particular stop at a travel plaza
for a franchise coffee and a franchise bagel
on the journey there. Just right it must be,
the faring out and its four hundred
and thirty miles. Thirsting for knowledge
with academics at the International
(amazing) Congress on Medieval Studies,
at last I arrive and unlock my room
—fit for a monk or a first-year student—
in a concrete cloister. Colleagues and friends
who are seldom seen are seen again,
all too briefly, as if in a dream.
Would some be closer if seen more frequently,
if endless roads or oceans vast
didn't sunder us? I soak in the experience,
yet terribly busy is the time at K'zoo:
so much unseen, so much unsaid.
But the magic and mystery of the Middle Ages
shines forth once more, in a form of sorts,
in papers and panels, and with plenty of wine.
A strange bird I am, but for the stretch that I'm here,
I'm a little less of a lone outsider.
Renewed I am for my needful quests
as skald and scholar. The schedule, however,
soon comes to an end, and so comes the time

for the road of return. A red T-shirt
is my pilgrim's badge, with a papal bull
as the central blazon. I'm soon back home,
in-between things in an outland realm,
a wilderness of sorts, where now it seems
a little more gray and my glowing lamp
is under a bushel. But onward I go
to new adventures and new strivings
and the going to K'zoo begins anew.

## Sometimes a Cigar Is Just a Poem

Freud is famous for phallic tobacco,
though he said at times it's simply not.
But maybe it's more than a mass of leaves,
brown and oily as if born from dirt.
Take from the top shelf this tube, for instance.
"Carpe Noctem" is its clever name,
insisting thus that you seize the night.
'Tis a multicultural mix in a magic wand:
from Pennsylvania, a pungent maduro
broadleaf wrapper, with binder and filler
from southern soil in sunny Nicaragua.
It is carefully aged, through art and craft,
for excellence truly isn't instantaneous.
A ritual begins this grand occasion:
one trims the cap (triple-layered)
and brings blue flame to burn the end.
Drawing deeply, a draught you'll get
of a fragrant herb fit for the gods,
not the scentless smell of the sorry realm
that cigarettes inhabit. And so we find
the urge to quality and artful leisure
in this hour-long smoke, endlessly complex.
A varied bouquet develops continually:
earth, oak, coffee, anise, chocolate,
leather, pepper, licorice, fruit,
and floral notes. Finding it all
would be a challenge. Better to soar
in these heights of quality, o'er a hell of quantity,

even if only at the odd occasion,
for sometimes a cigar, a symbol of potency,
is just a poem to enjoy with pleasure.

# Xicoy and the Heart

The call goes forth, the clamor resounds:
Return to the Heart! The time is at hand
for this holy work that'll heal the world.
And so Grails go forth, with the glory of Spirit
as shining emissaries to show the way.
From forests of rain, forth she has come,
cheerful Xicoy, the chocolate goddess,
carrying a secret of the Sacred Cup.
Kin to Óðrœrir, cousin of Absinthe,
her spirit is rare and especially hard
to find today. For found she is not
in the over-produced, endless supply
of modified candy that's manufactured
from deracinated beans into regular bars.
Don't get me wrong. It's good to eat;
the ordinary cacao is an excellent treat,
but severed was its link to the source of Spirit.
Something sacred was certainly lost
in the economies of scale that carried chocolate
to a hell of quantity, from the height of quality,
to a food of the masses, from a food of the gods.
So reserved she is for the zealous seekers
who Understand that the awesome power
in this magical plant from the Maya requires
careful cultivation and craft in producing
an heirloom variety of Criollo beans.
With a paucity of heat, the paste must be ground
to make the magical ceremonial grade.

Enjoy with reverence and joy as well
this primal strain in its purest form
of water and cacao, whisked together.
No sugar is required to sweeten the drink,
it is rich and delicious, just right as it is.
Allow her energy to alight in your heart,
expanding its space for Spirit's entry.
Heart Blood she is, and on a holy mission
to open our hearts to all that is love,
that we may come to know Condwir Amurs,
that Love Leads the Way, and go later on
to powerfully know Repanse de Schoye,
an Overflow of Happiness, and for all, compassion.
A shift is coming, led by shining Spirit,
with Xicoy's chocolate as a chosen emissary,
so know her anew in her needful drink
that's food for the shift, and find your way
in these times of trouble and Return to your Heart!

# Volcano

'Twas an empty land, only for grazing
and the occasional hike by a curious wanderer,
a beautiful valley of the barest acclaim.
But tremors abounded when the time was at hand,
as the hidden might of heat underground
steadily streamed, struggling to surface.
From far below this fire had surged:
mantle magma, unmixed with crust.
At last it erupts, and the lava flows.
In the arctic air, it inevitably cools
to a stream of stone, steel-gray in hue.
The steaming edges stand like a wall,
both heaped-up high and hastily jumbled,
yet slowly advancing, the sulfurous version
of glacier ice, greatly inexorable:
it creeps through the field, covering the valley.
But changes come in the chambers below,
and a second form soon emerges,
a fire geyser of frequent eruptions.
It's a mighty sight: the mountain's hot cum
vigorously spurts, a violent orgasm
of liquid fire and the land's baptism
for new growth and numberless possibilities.
But this too, shall pass, and in time enough,
the flow subsides, the fire diminishes,
the crater cools, and the cone is silent.
The new land sits, naked on earth,
in the endless cycles of seasons and weather

that gradually erode the rocks of gray,
taking an eternity to taper down
what formed so furiously in a fast eye-blink.

## Snowfall across the Worlds

All the events in the upper worlds,
even if ordinary, influence Midgard.
Mother Frau Holle is making her bed,
 shaking her blankets, shaking them vigorously,
and *we* get a blanket of the whitest snow.
The continual din of the day is tapered,
sound is suffocated by that snow-blanket,
and pure silence peals in powerful waves
across Midgard. We come to a halt,
our frenzy suspended in a forced rest;
an opportunity to take the measure
of our being and time 'gainst boundless nature.
The simple action of an ancestral goddess:
so commonplace, occurring frequently,
yet miraculous ever. Really, how else
could the wondrous worlds thus work together?

# Political

# Against Polarization and Hate

It's a world of hate, with war on all sides.
This eagle sorrows at the anger and hate,
pondering the problem from his perch in the tree.
What do you do if you do not hate,
when manifest multitudes are mandating hate?
Each end's extremes are stark-raving mad.
The ghost of McCarthy, that grim specter,
is haunting us still and hunting them out:
sometimes "communists," sometimes "fascists,"
depending on what the platform is.
Targets have changed, but tactics remain,
unjust as before and jury-lacking.
Witch-hunts, inquisitions, willful arrogance,
prideful disregard for due process,
and bashing people for the books they read.
That major villain, Matthew Hopkins,
would be very proud of the vicious mobs
and the awful "heroes" who emulate him.
The other end is not any better,
people-bashing 'gainst pigments of skin,
social safety-nets, sexual preferences,
and all who dare to organize labor
or aspire to other than spawning babies.
And both are prone to bloody violence:
senseless spectacles, signaling outrages,
tiki torches, taunting police,
anonymous threats on networked forums,
burning crosses, breaking windows,

suppressing speech, peddling intimidation.
Which end is which? The eagle wonders.
Was nothing learned from knowledge of history?
Really, making the "correct" choice
of others to other won't alter ourselves,
won't raise us up to a righteous standing.
A change of targets won't change consciousness,
won't make it evolve; a committed rising
above duality, above dark hate,
to the light above is the luminous path,
the only path, that goes up to Spirit.
Because, definitely, "darkness cannot
drive out darkness," deemed MLK,
"only light can do that"—only light, it's true.
And that "Hate cannot"—he said it best—
ever "drive out hate, only love can
do that." Damn right. The despotism now
of dualistic thinking is a difficult trap,
one that ensnares the world at large,
and even this eagle can only hope
that he is not trapped. But how to escape?
The willful seeker of serious wisdom
must start to drink from the strangest wells,
just like Óðinn, who journeys always
for value anywhere and avoids thus
the echo chambers on all of sides.
By blending many, the bright and the dark,
the inner and outer, the up and the down,
Óðinn obtains an artful synthesis,
for third alternatives and thoughtful solutions.

So aiming upwards, this eagle flies
—truly he does—with two of wings,
a left and a right. To live without hate,
he's stuck with both, for striving and flying.
Maybe you don't need such a matching pair,
especially if you're not a spirited flyer.
All us animals have our avenues to follow,
some on the ground, some in the sea,
some soaring up, and some elsewhere.
So own your journey as this eagle does his.

# I'm with Them

The supreme executive's power derives
from the masses' mandate, so a man has said.
But isn't that how we enabled this mess,
where the same-old same-old has ceased to work?
Could the status quo have stayed much longer?
When power comes from the people below,
no Lia Fáil will loose a roar
on the Capitol steps to sustain an election.
Far, far we've come from the first Capitol,
a temple of Jupiter in eternal Rome,
when a link to the sacred was a light for all.
'Tis a lucky accident for the beleaguered Occident
that's shaken things up. A shining opportunity
to seek a principle for replacing this swamp.
To see what's sought, we must certainly strive
for higher things and rehallow our world.
Then sparks of Spirit may speed again
to elect once more the leaders we need
in this atrophied land. So I'm with Them,
the distinguished maidens and the strange women
lying in ponds (in the living Waters),
distributing swords and establishing sovereignty:
the Eternal-Feminine o'er the Eternal-Empty.

## Make Yourself Great Again

Truly, creation is a time of chaos:
not petty disorder, but potential vast,
unmanifested, a magical void.
It's a time of chaos with Trump right now:
the media said it and mouthed it endlessly.
Will America be . . . made great again?
What about you, where do you fit?
Before you knew you, you were great once,
a spark in space of Spirit that shined
with a knowledge of Truth, but you needed experience.
So a womb you entered, with wondrous potential
and memories of the stars that made you strive.
Much you have used, no matter what,
of that great potential for growth in the world.
Nietzsche proclaimed that you needed chaos
for giving birth to a gamboling star.
Did you listen? Did you understand?
Chaos for a star: you've still enough
of your own material, unmanifested
—it's limitless, really, if you look enough—
deep in your Self. Dive for it now,
with speed from the spark of Spirit you have,
a gift of the gods who gave you life.
Only that chaos in your inner core
can reveal your purpose, your path to victory,
in the world today. Dare to find it,
and begin your creation, glorious and new,

to make your star and make yourself
great again now: you're gonna be YUGE!

# Ancient and Modern Dragons

Of ancient dragons, the elder poets
left us stories of their strength and size:
Of hungry Níðhögg, who gnaws at the roots
of the great green tree, a glorious ash
that nurtures the worlds, named Yggdrasil.
Of Jörmungand, who yields to none,
a serpent so big, he circled the world.
Of fierce Fáfnir, who was fought by Sigurð;
he hoarded gold in hubris and greed.
Their stories continue, still to this day,
as in Tolkien's tale of terrible Smaug,
that dread of dwarves when Dale he smote,
and famed Erebor followed after.
But dragons aren't real, else dead they're all.
Or are they really? Aim for the truth
behind the forms, hidden from sight,
and then you'll see how they have changed.
Today has dragons, those deadly fiends,
but green and scaly, their guise is not.
How do they look in these latter days?
They're media masters; our minds they fix,
limiting the space of allowed debate,
setting lie as truth and truth as lie,
gnawing the roots of needful inquiry.
They're mealy-mouthed and much deceitful
slimy politicians, who seek control
of every aspect in all our lives,
with power circling the people's world.

They're corporate Smaugs with cash they hoard
—like Fáfnir of old, on a field of gold—
wrecking the world with ruinous greed,
and terrorizing all who would take a coin.
So keep your courage in this Kali Yuga,
and for slaying dragons, seek old wisdoms,
for to face and defeat these fiercest terrors,
the days of old have dropped some hints,
though easy they aren't, to understand.
They speak of weapons, of special swords,
broken and reforged, for fame anew.
But what sword will slay a slimy corporation,
or make an end of media power,
or tame a congress of uncaring louts?
Best to be bold, brave, and fearless,
as Sigurð was, and so was Beowulf.
I know not now what knights will succeed
in slaying the dragons of this century's world,
but songs from poets they'll certainly earn,
like all who slew them in ancient days.

# The Conflict

Weapon's weather
waxes online,
war woods cast on the web:
does fire and ice
fuse in creation,
or in destructive storms of doom?

Can we feed the eagle
with our forceful words
and drive out hate with hate?
If they other others,
will othering them
bring a grant of Nike's gift?

Or can a bridge be built,
o'er the breach that's a canyon
to proffer a place at the table
and heal the hurt,
the hapless rage
and spawn a man of spit,

instead of jockeying
for the giant's labor
to be set between the sides,
encouraging each
to crush the other
as dehumanized unholy creatures
who dishonor the Æsir gods?

# Alliterative Sonnets

## Fire and Ice

Fire fiercely flickers, and fast it burns,
the purest Energy of a primal world;
for endless action it always yearns,
and racing around, it raged and swirled.
Ice is awe-filled and utterly still,
the purest Form of a primal realm;
'tis silent, focused, and centered will,
stopping motion with a steadying whelm.
Becoming and being: When blended, they're freeing.

# A Hanged Man

'Twixt the twain worlds, termed "New" and "Old,"
with a hard row to hoe, I'm hanged on this rock.
For soul's nourishment, I seek to hold
to my center within; of Self it's a stock.
The soil is strange here; I suffer a lack
of essential nutrients for my sorcerous tree,
but my quest continues, and I quit not this track.
With roots I reach for a requisite she,
and a flavor of heathens that's found not here,
and magical folk who feel the lights
of spirit o'er matter, who spurn what's mere:
a holy tribe with the hearts of knights.
My struggle continues; I strive for deeds,
while aiming for balance with an eye to my needs,
to gain my goals and grow my seeds.
Hanged on myself, with hope I stand,
to finish my thesis, fully as planned,
and dream of new life in a distant land.

# Iceland as Thule

I write of Thule and the runes it may hold,
for I've quested there to quicken my life
and study its skalds and their storied gold,
to sharpen my mind like a shiny knife.
Strange is Iceland, and I've stayed a while
in this alien terrain, aiming to live
as best I can on this boon-filled isle
—weird is its spirit—for what it can give.
'Tisn't Hyperborea—it's heavily wind-swirled—
but a Muse is present in this magical land
that's beyond the borders of the habitual world,
especially in the aurora that's regal and grand.
Noble North-ness is knowable here,
found aplenty in the fire and ice;
interminable night, by turning year,
to midnight sun, is a sacrifice.
Seek the synthesis of such and more,
for the rightful runes of this realm of Thor.

# Industry and Sloth

Rest I desire, yet reach for deeds:
an inner struggle 'twixt industry and sloth.
Poles of a spectrum, these are opposing needs:
I synthesize them with serious troth.
With might and main on many a quest
of poetry and scholarship, I patiently work.
Diligent deeds I dare with zest,
but needful duties I must never shirk.
Yet after slack I always seek,
time to idle and take a pause,
to let things go, make light for a week,
and feel some peace to fight the blahs.
To blend them both is my balancing test,
that each must feed the other in turn
—with wode, with words, with work, with rest—
so that my inner fire will always burn.
Sloth and striving: I seek these extremes,
their runes are needed to realize my dreams.

# The Odian Wanderer

Mysteries exist, their magic is real!
The Odian Wanderer must always seek
for such unknowns and the secrets they reveal,
to gain in gnosis from getting a peek.
His example is Óðinn, the eldest god,
who hung on the Tree, harrowed by gar;
the Runes he gained, their road he trod.
With that treasure won, he's traveled far!
The Wanderer emulates Óðinn in quest,
and seeks inside the soul of his tree,
for memory's might with mindful zest,
and the focused thought that forms the key.
The Wanderer travels the world outside:
hidden corners he hopes to find,
terrors and marvels he takes in stride,
crossing borders that curb and bind.
The Wanderer learns from living flesh:
plants and animals, and the powers they teach;
women and men, and the way they mesh;
and the force of life and its fimbul speech.
The staves are the guides! Those stalwart signs
give lore for finding the polarities in all
—with the mead of inspiration in its many wines—
to unseal the mysteries and receive their haul.
With puissance he wanders through plenty of moons,
growing always—for the greatest of boons—
in might and main by means of the Runes!

# Esotericism

# Moldavite: Stone and Grail

The Grail is real, and it's green to boot.
Found in Czechland, famed Moldavite,
the Jewel of Moldau, is a joyous stone,
Vltavín to the locals, and valued for centuries.
This star-born stone is a stately green,
unique 'mongst tektites, those noble pebbles
made only by the aid of the heavens.
'Twas made in an Age of Elder Time
ere Europe today was yet to be,
when a fimbul fire from far above
—perhaps 'twas green with holy splendor—
blazed in the sky and blasted the earth
in terror and glory. Much time would pass
for the stones that were made and strewn about
ere they reached the now. To the realm of the gods
we must look to learn what legends came forth
for its legacy today and the light it carries.
Was it war in heaven that worked that gift
of the deepest green which dropped from the sky,
a loosened gem from Lucifer's crown,
that Parzival would win through plenty of questing,
the glorious Grail of greatest renown?
Or permanent pieces of the plasma glow
from the Northern Lights that were needfully made
into polar stones for the peoples of the North,
a boon and hallow from Hyperborea?
Christian culture had called gemstones
the precious overflow of Paradise's rivers.

What place might it've given to this puzzling emerald?
The Norse did too give noble things
a godly origin. Glowing amber
was Freyja's tears. Fire became gold,
Ice became silver in the idiom of myth.
Could Moldavite be, in a myth that was lost,
the Heart of Hrungnir, that hallowed stone
that Thor had won in a thunderous duel?
Hermes Trismegistus, that hallowed Sage
had an Emerald Tablet with all his wisdom,
maintaining the secrets of the Hermetic Art.
Might Moldavite be that mystic tablet?
What mysteries are within its magical depths?
'Tis an alchemist's Stone, as that ancient cataclysm
of terrific power made the twain unite,
both dry the Earth and dry the Fire,
in a principle entity that's proffered not
otherwise else in ordinary Nature.
Could someone past have seen it as
"the simple-seeming unsought-for Stone
that indeed in value is deemed a trifle,
detested by fools but treasured by the wise?"
'Cause after all, to eyes that see
at the lowest level—the level of fools—
it is merely glass, this mighty stone.
But with higher sight that is heart-centered,
its occult virtues may come to be known.
It's a Solar stone: it has the Sun within,
a bright Black Sun of brilliant Spirit.
Allied with Gold, it links to Gold,

and 'tis Gold as a gem with a greenish hue.
The heart it opens to higher realities
to spur one's Ascent on a spiritual path,
dry and magical. Deeply meditate
on this Sign from Spirit, and then seek Spirit.
But beware always, for your wyrd it'll alter,
bringing changes and breaking routines.
But boons will come if you brave it through,
and help perhaps, for healing yourself
and the Wounded King and Wasteland barren.
In finding Moldavite, thus find you will
the Stone and the Grail, a most strange gem;
your Quest may end. Then your Quest will begin.

# The Emerald Tablet

The truth, sans untruth, most true and certain:
As below thus above, as above thus below,
these make when unified the miracles of the One.
All things are One, and all things, by Work
and Rework of the One, from the One they come.
'Tis sired and mothered by Sun and Moon,
waxed in Wind's womb, and wet-nursed by Earth.
All the world's works of wonder it causes;
its power is whole, complete, and entire.
If to earth it is turned, then earth and fire
are separated surely, and the subtle from the gross,
when acting with care and artful wisdom.
It ascends from earth, it descends from heaven,
and united thus, 'tis naturally the lord
over the above and over the below.
You gain this way the glory of the world,
and out thus drive all of darkness.
'Tis the force o'er forces that fulfills mastery:
the subtle it subdues, the solid it penetrates.
Thus the micro accords with the macro in the cosmos,
and the world entire in this way was formed.
Wonders manifold do wax from it,
manifested hence by the means here given.
Thus here I'm called Hermes, Thrice-Greatest,
unifying the three parts of universal philosophy.
This is the sum entire of the Solar Work.

# Total Solar Eclipse

So seldom seen by the sundry peoples,
a total eclipse of Terra's sun
is an "awesome event," in all the senses
of that phrase's morphemes, former and modern.
Recently now, in a rare occurrence
with the grandest style, the Great American
Solar Eclipse bisected the country;
from sea to sea the sun went dark.
We know the material and temporal science
of why it occurs, but what beyond
are the higher meanings of this hallowed sight
and its upward opening to the awe of Spirit?
A truth is told by a tale of the lore
of elder times when all was young:
*Máni þat né vissi hvat hann megins átti*,
"Máni knew not what main he had."
Yet much of main does Máni have,
shining at night, but surely more
in the shadow self he seldom shows
as blackest Sköll, a bounding wolf
who criss-crosses the course of Sól,
silently chasing her slender form
and visible only when victory looms.
Árvakr and Alsviðr are always straining
to keep a pace that's clear of Sköll,
but every so often, their efforts fail
and Sköll succeeds; thus a skald had said:
*Sól tér sortna*, "the Sun turns black."

In deepest azure, the darkness falls
as the shining disc shrinks to a gleam,
an enthralling diamond on an ethereal ring.
That gleam of Sól is soon engulfed;
it occurs in a moment, that consummation,
and fire flares forth as a fimbul crown
on that awesome orb, that onyx jewel,
giving a glimpse, glorious yet brief,
of the true black sun of the timeless realm,
and the flow of awe will fill your core,
as a surge of Spirit descends from above.
Immerse in that marvel, but make it creative
by wielding it also for works of magic.
Both Óðinn's eyes are in awesome union,
the eye in the Well and the eye in the Tree,
so that Well and Tree are one thus briefly
for a sacred time of singular power.
That might and main, a Master longs
to see and know, to seize the supernal.
With waxing wonder, the one chants out,
between two worlds in a twilight zone,
so that the fire of wode will flame within
and the magic of moments will mark an Age.
No sooner it's done than Sól returns
and bit by bit is reborn as she died.
Or is it her daughter that dazzles forth
in the light renewed on the lands below?
An eclipse gives not its arcana otherwise
than seeing it live, a sight in person,
as a mortal in the fourfold, facing divinity

'twixt earth and sky, open to Being
and acting with a Will to awe and wonder.
It is a Ragnarök that readies one
for a bright rebirth with the blessings of Spirit
as triumph is illumined by returning light.
So seek for yourself that singularity
and the fimbul runes that fill such a time,
for Máni's shadow has a mighty power
to consecrate the core of a soul
in those sacred moments of solar death.

# Triadic Experiences

*Rúna Experience*
In a summer of seeking the secret mysteries
through structured work with the stalwart Runes,
the flash came suddenly, in a fiery blaze,
that Óðrœrir was real, that this awesome Mead
existed in the worlds for the zealous seeker
to win, drink, and pour: the wealth of poetry,
yet the mighty substance of magic also,
a mainful treasure truly 'yond measure.

*Wode Experience*
"An Óðr to the fire, for Óðr from the fire!"
This evolving skald sought a victory debut
at a campfire contest with a crafted poem.
Both will and work were well aligned,
and the channel opened, with charged mead filling
my entire being; I truly changed
and the fiercest fire then flowed from my tongue,
pouring Óðrœrir into the people's ears.

*Grail Experience*
For good long years, the Grail had beckoned
with the promise of Ascent and the power of Spirit;
then its road was made by the Runes and Mead
when I answered the call to offer stanzas
for its heathen hallows. A holy essence
then flooded my being with fimbul duty
to the Grail and its Quest, an unquenchable fire
that invested me fully with a vigorous Knighthood.

# Sonnenrad or So-Called "Black Sun"

The zig-zagging Sonnenrad icon,
that solar symbol that's set in the floor
of the north tower of that noble castle
called Wewelsburg, provokes the souls
of many people with its mighty power.
Fear and fury and foaming mouths
greet the attempts to gainsay the censure
that the Establishment has esteemed for it.
Others are moved to anger and hate
in revolt against a valueless world
both proper and post, of depraved modernity,
but blindly act with the barest perception.
But what would we do, if we didn't have
the chattering classes to choose for all
and set the sooth of the symbol's meaning?
Where might free-thinkers, who don't follow herds,
start their study of this un-storied sign?
What mystery is here, what main does it have?
Let's look with eyes for the light unseen,
and start with the details of that strange symbol,
to shine the sun on this shadowy mystery.
Gold-set originally, with green stone around,
it's not black at all, though "Black Sun" it's called
in the world today. But what before
was its name and purpose? Unknown they remain,
lost to history, leaving us all
to fill in the blanks and find a meaning.
Of Sig runes twelve it's said to be made,

but right that isn't. They're really backwards,
an cryptic form that's kenned as Zil,
devised by Wiligut for a variant futhark.
Here it is Ziel, a Hochdeutsch word:
aim, goal, target, object, and purpose.
Thus this that's sent, and thence outwards.
But out from where? An *axis mundi*
was the intended aim of that enterprise,
a center of the world, set in Westphalia.
Any such center is sorely lacking
in the Western world, but wanted by many
in these rootless times on the right and left.
But why then twelve? Let's wax mythic:
Twelve for the knights, twelve for the apostles,
twelve for the Aesir, twelve for the zodiac?
The King at the center—Christ or Arthur—
or glorious Valhalla or the Grail itself?
But notice the rings, that are numbered two,
enclosing it. The closer one
is a corona perhaps, or the Round Table.
The outer, then, is the edges of the world,
that the shimmering sun shines to illumine.
Both ways go the paths: winding they are
and never straight, though numbered twelve.
Reversed, 'tis by Sig to venture on them;
by sun and victory a seeker may travel.
But why then green, what's the meaning?
The Northern Lights are the nighttime mystery
of the daytime sun. Dare it be this?
But why the shape? What are the roots?

'Tis an evolved manifestation of Merovingian disks,
a fusion of history and hidden inspirations.
This "black" business is the bit that's left,
a later accretion to the legend, but why?
Below the Absolute, on the level we're at,
their own opposites, all things contain.
So *sol niger* was certain to attach
to this known unknown that needed completion.
How does Modernity deal with the symbol?
People fear power, and powerful it is,
so this dispassionate look that ponders the symbol
will be roundly condemned by the rabid dogs
of knee-jerk nastiness and needless hate,
and an intelligentsia, jaundiced and trite,
that fears and despises, on flimsiest grounds,
mythopoetic motivation as a major heresy,
instead of wielding such stuff itself.
What do they see? What they all bring.
Haters gonna hate. What should heroes do,
those who deem today Tradition their guide?
The poet ponders the purest essence,
the hidden mysteries that hearken back
to the Ideal form, the *Dasein* untainted
by petty human prejudiced attachments,
to gain a glimpse of the greater world
that has Nobility, Truth, Beauty, and Spirit
to bring these back to beings in the world.
The Forest Rebel, in forging meaning,
must make his own *axis mundi*,
hidden inside his heart as a guide

for shining outwards his surest purpose.
The daring alchemist aims to make gold,
seeking to transmute, *solve et coagula*,
indeed must transmute, matter that's base;
stasis, stagnation, is instead the alternative.
So here's a "black sun" to hallow to gold,
and a sign for a Center to set within,
and a symbol to seek for a Solar ideal.

*Author's Note: I wrote this preceding poem in 2020 as I was first becoming fascinated with the symbol. I had not yet had the full revelation of its true identity that I would have in 2025. I considered rewriting it to reflect that revelation. Instead, I felt it best to let this poem stand as is—a testament to the development of my thought and that I took my own advice in seeking its mysteries. So I composed the following poem in honor of the symbol's true identity.*

# Round Table Sun Wheel

In Castle Wewelsburg, there's a curious symbol
in the North Tower at the intended Center;
in troubled times, this token was laid
and worked in marble of white and green.
Great was its hall, for housing the Grail,
and green are its columns, the color given
by Wolfram's tale as the worthiest setting.
'Twas a mystery made from the mind of Wiligut
at Himmler's behest for his highest officers,
to lift them up as a living knighthood,
to equal the best that were bearing arms
for famed King Arthur in former days.
Fashioned as a fusion of fabled legends
—the art and lore of Arthur's Knights—
and the intriguing discs that are deemed Zierscheibe,
it's the Round Table that's rightly bounded
by the outer ring and inner ring
of this solar wheel that swirls on the floor.
Twelve Zil runes are arrayed on the Table
—the swords of the Knights that serve the realm—
reaching to the circle, right in the middle,
that is a shining halo with the surest core:
the Holy Grail of hallowed legend,
the aim and goal of those angled swords.
'Twas once depicted with a wondrous treasure,
a golden disk, but go there now,
and only a substitute of off-color marble
—the Grail's shadow and green also—

remains to be seen by the masses today.
Round Table Sun Wheel is the rightful name
of this symbol designed for a serious purpose.
It is art made icon, to energize Ascent,
to challenge the viewer to choose the Quest,
needful for knights to ennoble their being:
gaining the Grail and its glories many.
But the Black Order had a brutal heart
that heeded not the hallowed tales
that told us all the truth of the Quest,
of the worthiness required by one who would seek.
So they found no favor from the forces of Spirit
they invoked in the tower by that valiant symbol.
Brutal violence turned back to crush them,
and their Grail Castle of great Wewelsburg
was stripped from them. But secreted away
was that golden disk, the Grail for Himmler,
and lost it is now, for it has left the world,
no prize for people to pillage as a trophy,
whether Axis or Allies or other allegiance.
The Round Table remains, for right it was
that none should destroy such a noble sign
of Tradition's light in our darkening world.
Our task today is of the tallest order,
and only for the few who'd aim for Ascent:
to fulfill the challenge that was failed by Himmler
and truly be worthy of this token of Spirit
for gaining the Grail, again once more.

# Et in Arcadia Ego

Where is Arcadia? What is Arcadia?
These are fair questions for finding answers.
But most important is the message it has.
Forests of Spirit are found in that land
which lets beings be to bear their Truth.
The trees have deep roots: tall they will grow,
to touch the sky in triumph and Ascent.
Runes aplenty are readily grasped;
they lay on the ground for lifting up.
You'll find in Arcadia the forest whence
Askur and Embla came ørlög-lacking
to the ancient shore where Óðinn shaped
their wondrous wyrd. In wide rivers,
there are precious fluids pouring in torrents:
the blood of heroes, the bright mead of poets,
and the ink of scholars. The skaldic eagles
are wending whither these wonders are;
with zeal they seek the zenith above.
The Absolute here is ever-present:
the All in all and All beyond,
which is nothing like "the night in which
all cows are black." Au contraire, blindness,
a lack of light, cannot lift the veil
of higher Truth. In its holy synthesis,
through joy the system of German Idealism
is complete at last. Apollo's spirit
and Óðinn's energy are omnipresent
in this Hyperborean High-Atlantis,

and the Grail is gained. The great roads thither
are individuation and actualization:
become who you are, the craft of the Self.
You can ponder the painting from Poussin's brush,
but you need not seek the noble tomb
of a storied god whose stead is unknown,
as some suggested. But they're certainly right
that the secrets of gods are concealed in Arcadia.
When you gain the gnosis of its glorious trees
—via Mead or Runes or Royal Art—
in wisdom you'll know, as one who sees,
that on Earth Arcadia is only in the Heart.

# Hyperborea: The Polar Seat

Hail Polyhymnia! Of Hyperborea,
that celestial land that was lost to time,
inspire me to speak with spirited verse.
Beyond the North Wind is this noble land,
a holy realm that was hiding away
in the *terra incognitae* of times long gone,
but no such land is now remaining.
What might have been the main of its being
in the Golden Age when gods still ruled?
In that archipelago, an island realm,
the cold came not, and 'twas calm and sunny.
At this polar seat, Apollo is highest,
with a sacred precinct and a solar temple.
The people esteem the practice of arts
for powerful prophecy, poetry, and music;
always the Muses are all around.
They live very far from labor and battle,
their sacred lives unsullied by disease,
bitter old age, or baseless fears.
In the Central City, it is sacred to live.
The sun circles 'round at summer's height
in an endless day that's all of six months.
At the depth of winter, in the dreamy night,
the wondrous stars are wheeling about
with the gods' green lights in a glorious dance.
Yet even in darkness, it is always warm.
The Central Tower sits on the axis,
an ever-reminder of the awesome duty

of ruling right where the world spins around.
In that realm ere time, the rest of the globe
was stark and strange. Stifling heat
was south of that seat in searing deserts
and sweltering jungles, while seas were rough;
for most of humanity, 'twas a mean existence.
Yet allegiance they had to an uplifting mission,
so ere their occultation, they were out in the world;
their light and legends they allowed to be known.
At Delos and Delphi, they ordained great shrines.
And that Hyperborean, the healer Abaris,
traveled the world, trained in medicine
for both soul and body. We've a serious need
for his healing today—our hapless souls
are sick of modernity and seek for a cure.
The lights of Tradition yet linger on,
signs for the seekers that the ascended ones left.
So look to Polaris, the luminous aurora,
and the Noble North for the needful tokens
and holy boons that the Hyperboreans
have left to guide the long ages
of the world's existence till their wondrous return.

# Call to the "Rosicrucians"

Of the "Rosicrucians" and their curious runes,
I speak now in verse, but must name them clearly:
the mysterious original, started in Europe
in the seventeenth century, a secret Order,
is the group at hand, not what goes after.
They've a curious venue, an Invisible College,
a brick building with budding wings
for soaring upwards to seek for Spirit
and a base with wheels, a benefit to a guild
that's always on the move in offering its wisdom.
A sword defends 'gainst seekers unworthy,
and a trumpet's blast attends its passage
for the few with the ears, a fortunate elite,
to hear its message of holy renewal
to the panoply of arts and a path to wisdom.
Defenders on ramparts face all directions,
watching for friends, watching for foes.
No particular garments they prided in wearing,
but in lands they occupied, the customs they followed.
Wanting seekers as worthy successors,
call to them, they said, and call many did.
But none were answered—none that said so:
"Those who say don't know; those who know don't say."
Their weird College, where could it be?
Everywhere, really, and also nowhere.
Though that time-bounded, temporal manifestation
was lost to history (yet it left some traces),
its Spirit lives on, a spark that's reborn

anew in the world in new lights,
time after time for true Initiates.
'Tis a Golden Thread that gamboled through the Ages,
even long before that limited appearance
in the seventeenth century. The Solar essence
of that august fraternity is the ever-constant
beacon of Tradition, bearing renewal.
In multiple garments—Masonry, Alchemy,
Gnosis, Yoga, Knighthood, Runes, et cetera—
it has made its mark and manifests still.
So if you're a seeker, then a search begin.
They're here today, dressed in the forms
that suit the time of this sundered-from-Spirit,
all-too Modern World. Make your revolt;
your eyes and ears you must open wide,
and center yourself in your Self's true heart.
Their bona fide heirs are found by their boons
where Mysteries are sought, the Mead is poured,
and Ascent is the way. Seek that College
with eyes of the heart and ears of the heart,
and you just might chance some joyful perceptions:
its passage to see and its approach to hear
as it rolls through Midgard, roaming the world
and blowing its trumpet to attract the worthy.
Thus, make your call, most sincerely
—if you're really ready—to the "Rosicrucians,"
appropriate to your nature and with pure intent.
And perhaps you'll find the help of both,
an answer from them and an offer that's rare:
to gainfully join with the Golden Thread,

linking with Tradition for the light of renewal
and a wisdom path in the world today.

The Invisible College of the Rose Cross Fraternity

# Personal

# The Black Dog

A poem now I compose this time
on that darkest haze, a draining of color
from my view of the world, the vigor-killer
that's called depression. It's a constant pet
that I can't be rid of, though it can be leashed,
and sometimes it sleeps. He said it best,
that war leader, Sir Winston Churchill,
when naming it thus a nasty Black Dog.
The Dog has a multitude of dreary forms.
In earlier times, this odd temperament
was mostly called melancholy,
and thought to be an imbalance of humors,
caused by black bile being in excess.
About such bile, I barely know,
but on the saddest of days, it seems to involve
another fluid that's known to be black:
it's like moving through a molasses sea.
I feel it also in other forms:
like limbs waylaid with leaden weights
(the hound on my back, holding tightly),
or an urge to idleness for endless time
(like a dog in summer, drooping in the heat).
At times I'm trapped in the tomb of my head,
with thoughts racing and thudding around.
It's a slowing down of myself to the world,
which is racing by, with the relentless ticking
of the "real-time clock" as a ruthless oppressor,
while I'm standing still and stuck in a rut.

"Pause" I would press on the passage of time,
and sit for hours, or sit for days,
relieved of burdens till the listlessness passed.
Myself I drive to soar to the heights,
too hard at times, perhaps I do.
Some tools I try to retain my center:
galdor and herbs to gladden the Dog
—when it's growling and weighing me down—
and meditation to steer my mind from within.
Or alchemical work to alter my state,
as black bile and blood can balance together:
melancholia—'tis cold and dry—
mixes with sanguine—'tis moisture and warmth.
But for this chimerical Dog, I must constantly
shift my methods; a sure balance
is only found in a chaotic manner.
Sometimes I need to set it loose,
allowing it freedom and letting it run
till it gets tired and takes a nap.
What truly works? I wish I knew.
In all the methods, my aim must be
to form a friendship with this fearsome Dog
—since, after all, it's always present—
and train it well for trust and weal
with collar, leash, and quality biscuits.
For it actually is, in this incarnation,
a part of me, and repudiating it
would work as well as willingly repressing
my shadow self. To shine from my center,
my eternal task is Transmutation,

and no exception this certainly is.
Hail the Black Dog. Who's a good boy?

# Beautiful Darknesses

In the Grail legend's greatest telling,
chastity is not a needed choice.
The Lord of the Grail is allowed a woman,
whose name appears in numinous script
in flames on its surface. Unfree he is
to have another. (Now, try he can,
but that course of action does not climax well.)
I quest for the Grail, that quickening hallow,
but by binding myself to that boldest endeavor,
perhaps I'm doomed to have that fate:
those who truly commit to that trying quest
become a Grail Lord in a kind of way.
But a life's reflection of the legend's truth
is seldom clear, and we simply cannot
assume identical sexual constraints.
What Grail guidance is given to me?
Which women when? What circumstances?
I seek a glimpse of my Grail inside,
but uncloudy visions of the occult realms
still elude me. Striving anyway,
I try what I can, testing for gnosis.
So I must sense, seeking to know,
and years of reflection have yielded insights
on my ideal women who are deemed by the Grail,
that love I should seek in lights of darkness.
It's weird ones, always—and "wyrd" especially—
that catch my eye and curious heart.
Normal and ordinary will never do.

They all, it seems, have an outer "darkness"
in personal style. They've pride of a kind
and a strong individuality with extreme intelligence.
Not bumbling with herds, they blaze their own trails:
creative spirits with an urge for expression,
distinguished, introspective, with strong inner life.
The "little skald," a scholar like me,
captured my heart in cold Iceland;
her name had blazed on the noble Grail
for the sweetest of times. Those times have passed;
will they turn again? Yet treasure remains:
the mead of memories of moments so precious.
Others with fire, my eyes they caught.
All have darkness in their inner depths.
I wanted their names to wax in the flames,
of the gleaming Grail, but the grace came not.
Some I will say, concealed in staves.
A sassy smart lass with a smile was one,
genuine darkness in a jaunty devil.
Another was confused, full of anguish,
blinded by pain—she was beautiful once
to me for a moment. Maybe my light
burned her harshly; did it brighten a corner
that she'd keep in the dark? (I can't see my light,
but a certain few insist it's there.)
A third is fierce, yet full of tenderness,
with grim cold fire as a *galdrakona*,
a full paradox that befits a seeker.
A fourth so talented, I fancied greatly,
an alpine darkness with an air exotic

and heart that's kind behind a mask
of pain and pride, a pretty artist.
A fifth an artist, so fiercely weirdest,
has a voice as deep as the volume is loud
of the booming waters of her borderland home.
Others could be also named here,
but these are a few and they'll suffice.
Of these wished-for ones, what really of them?
The work of wyrd in wispy glimmers,
from lives in the past, or lives in the future?
Missed opportunities? Imagined opportunities
that were just vain hopes? I journey onward,
and the alchemist's task—the aim to transmute—
I must perform with those missed connections
to release the lust to alight anew
in my sexual searching for a serious partner.
I need perhaps another quality
in a woman to share my world and life.
One who is burdened, with wisdom like me,
to see how horribly, horribly complex
the world is now, that it needs the Grail,
the Mead of Poetry, and the mighty Runes
to re-make sacred Midgard today.
And so I seek, and so I call
for a light of darkness, a lover with spirit,
to find me here, and the flaming of her name
in runic script to read on the surface
of the glorious Grail. But by growth and quest,
can its grace be influenced and given a nudge?
Or are its choices governed by chance alone?

Always and ever, in all of this,
Mystery remains, as mysteries I seek,
and some of the sweetest, in sex and love.

# Fertility

Always creative is the act of sex,
frequently forming, in the physical world,
a new life to join the never-ending cycle
that links the ancestors to their line of descendants.
It's creative also in other ways
and on other planes—astral, etheric,
mental, and beyond—a mystery to seek.
But a living child, a legacy of blood,
is not for me; on another path
is my Work in this world—it is one of discipline,
yet sex-celebrating in the search for Spirit.
With the help of holiness, my human fertility
was changed with two cuts; my choice overdue.
A week-long wound, worked in the "thighs,"
like the Fisher King, but with forceful intent;
not the base pursuit of banal pleasure
as he once did, heedless of his calling,
but a final acceptance of my Form within,
that my Path and Work have no procreation,
but creation alone: in arts and letters,
a legacy of inspiration, not of living flesh.
It is orienting also my afterlife path
to the Olympian leap of luminous heroes
instead of return in a string of descendants.
My seed is no longer sent in the world,
but is focused inward to fertilize my soul,
while a sterile cum streams from my cock.
A modern mystery, a magic of Ingwaz,

a runic rerouting to realize Jera,
the copious harvest, in a peculiar way,
while still embracing the strong energies
of the Serpent power through sexual pleasure
to soar as an Eagle in Ascent and joy.

# Farewell

From black winter nights
through brightening spring,
you've been my lifting light.
I hail you, Lucie,
with these heartfelt staves
for our time together in Garður
and an awesome year in Iceland.

As we wander on
and wax in glory,
I'll treasure the time we've shared.
Let our spirits get speed
from the sparks we kindled
as we wend to meet our wyrds,
in the world that's out from Iceland.

The road joined us
and the road parts us
but on it goes to Asgard;
may we reach Valhöll
with righteous victories
and many happy memories
and toast together with the gods.

## Luciidrápa

O Lucie, my lady,
our layers together
in the Well of Wyrd
were the work of norns
and giving gods
with a great interest
in blessing our lives
with brightest joy.

Meeting at first
in the Medieval North,
with your stellar smile,
you stirred my heart.
At semester's end
we merged at last
in delightful kisses
in that lofty attic.

In Gamli Garður,
together we were;
in that enchanted land
you charmed my heart:
beneath the aurora,
next to the ocean,
and in winter dark
with white snow cover.

Together we were steered
by the graces of wyrd.

*Our time I'll remember
and treasure always.*

Standing atop
Stóri-Dímon,
and going swimming
at the lagoon of legend
—with passionate embraces
in that polar land—
together we were
as degrees we sought.

In Oslo also,
at the end of my degree
you were there with me
when then I enjoyed
summer celebrations
and the solar peak;
coupled once more
we cleaved together.

We were hand in hand
o'er hills and islands,
along the lake,
and lurking in forests.
It all I would do
yet over again,
despite the sorrows
of our splitting twice.

You were great to me
when together were we.
*Our time I'll remember
and treasure always.*

You always believed,
ever-confident,
in my scholarly skills
and skaldic quests,
dispelling the doubts
that appeared in my heart:
a life-giving tonic
for my lengthy struggles.

Skáldið litla,
your skillful verses
put spring in my spirit
and sparks in my heart.
May Bragi always
bless your verses
with the magic mead
of the Mighty Þulr.

Praises I've sung
and proffered now,
from skald to skald,
great scholars both.
May this mead of mine
and the mighty gods
ever aid you
in all that you do.

Till we meet again,
let's remember what's been,
our together-time
in a gladsome prime.

# Tide

'Twas an unlikely time for lust to strike,
at the looming end of my Icelandic adventure,
when my soon-departure had been set already,
but we proved to be the pairing we needed.
A match on an app, messages for a time,
and meeting for beer. I saw much to like.
Spiritual a bit, you aspire to art,
with an eye toward the old masters.
Brown luscious hair and blue pale eyes
—with silver circles inside the iris—
accentuate your form, sensuous and graceful,
and its feminine features are full and abundant.
You liked me too; luck was with us,
we both got lucky, for we both were hungry.
Our four nights together, too few they were,
but in three of them, our thirst was magical
and our times of trysting truly made Mead,
like Gunnlöð and Óðinn, in this goodbye adventure.
The entire experience is intensely spiritual,
a true encounter with Transcendent Beauty,
from first to last, foreplay to cuddling.
We devour each other with vigorous kissing,
mouths in a frenzy, moaning with hunger,
loosening clothes, longing to feel
warm skin on skin with skillful touches.
With bare bodies and building anticipation,
the kissing continues and my cock hardens.
Your flesh, naked, is a feast for my eyes,

as I slip inside your most sacred space.
My delight is magnified in a mix of positions
 as I fondle your tits, while fucking your pussy;
I'd thrust forever if my thorn could manage.
The luminous mystery of our love-making
fills my being, and its forms are many.
Sexual bliss is in the scent of your body,
the feel of your center firmly around me,
and our heat, yearning, heaving, and groaning.
The burning desire brings us higher,
again and again, to our glorious cummings,
and we abandon ourselves to the boundless rapture.
Cuddling in afterglow, close together
our fires stay hot for further unions,
til finally we're spent and falling asleep.
The spirit remains, though the moments have passed,
and in my inner soul, Erato sings
of the treasured memories of our times together.
In sex is seen both, the transcendent and vulgar,
but for channeling focus, the choice is ours,
though needful it is to acknowledge both.
An Ideal to pursue now dwells within me,
for future partners, for finding poetry,
and for opening my soul to the sacred in all.

# Ærdna

A brief flutter that barely fizzled
on a meeting app would be mostly forgotten,
but a second chance may sometimes happen,
and you were the one that worked that "yes."
After summer's end, you sought a meeting;
at my thesis defense you thoughtfully listened,
and at the cellar joined the celebration later.
A determined spirit, you continued on
for further festivities at the famed Ölstofan;
we smoked cigars and sipped our drinks.
More yet we'd meet, in the remaining time
ere I left Iceland for my olden life.
Your green-gold eyes were glowing with warmth
o'er a tender smile that touches the heart.
Friendly, philosophical, and full of kindness,
holding to Kant and human dignity,
you adored my autism and diverse quirks.
Together three nights, we gladdened our hearts
as we shared ourselves, though too short the time.
A saunter on the beach was a sweet memory,
and a farewell lunch finished our time.
But on my way to the airport, 'twas a welcome surprise
when you boarded by chance the bus I was on,
for farewell kisses and final goodbyes.
I returned to the 'States, but we stayed in touch,
through video calls and virtual hugs
and digital beers with a dash of emojis.
Your caring and kindness would keep me inspired

as I aligned o'er time to life outside
the academia I knew. I dreamed of return,
and our chats reminded that choice to me.
But a summer of travel would see us briefly
rejoined for a festival when I journeyed to Norway.
Hand in hand, happy, we heard the music
together at the blót, the best of gatherings.
In the nights again, we knew each other,
our limbs entwined and lips caressing
in the searing lust of sexual embrace.
We parted again, yet in pleasant mind,
continuing our chats o'er time and space.
Generous, supportive, joyful, and tender,
I will always remember and amiably think
of your luminous heart of loving kindness.

# Fire, Ashes, and Rebirth

The phoenix is famous for its fiery death,
for when burnt to ashes, it is reborn anew.
'Tis a great talent, and good to have,
but imagine how painful that method must be.
A mite more than others, such misery I know
from the blazes that burned my bare skin harshly.
A ritual celebration went wrong extremely;
on New Year's Eve, the nascent fire
of sacred intent went surging out
of its proper pot to imperil myself.
What woeful wyrd had worked this bale?
Hot-headedness within became harrowing without?
'Twas soon extinguished, but not soon enough.
The liquid fire, alight on my flesh,
caused sores and harm in seconds flat.
Thus burnt to "ash," I was borne to an "underworld,"
the liminal realm of a local hospital;
my wounds were treated, then the waiting began.
I lay in a daze, a little death,
resting in a small room. A range of people,
many masked faces, would make their rounds.
But time did pass, and I returned home,
just partly healed, but judged sufficient.
The brief respite was blissful indeed;
home is sweeter when the heart desires it.
But the fire of *kaun*, with a fierce swelling,
lurked in my leg and lingered yet on.
So barely a week, then back to the underworld:

my infected flesh needed further treatment.
A new wound I got, worked in my thigh,
for fresh clean flesh to fill the burns
after the hide's corruption was hacked from my leg.
Free of infection, I was finally released,
for the long recovery while my life continued.
Through weeks of recovery I waited patiently,
like the wondrous phoenix that wants rebirth.
But bit by bit, I was reborn anew,
a phoenix eagle, to fly again.
*Phoinix* in Greek is defined also
as "reddish purple," rightly appropriate
for the hue of my burns as their healing continues—
this phoenix skald now has *phoinix* skin.
The scabs fell off, but the scars will remain,
though pressure garments deplete them much
o'er many long months of committed wearing.
A red right "hand," a relic of the occasion,
is one of those gloves that I wear often.
I feel yet still that fire lingering,
in the tingle of nerves, in the twinge on my knuckles,
where they laid the grafts on my leg and hand.
Whether 'twas wanted, it's worked transformation
in my self and Self in a serious way.
I'm wiser at least, or one so hopes.
Was the fault that led to the fire burned out
of me by the fire? Maybe it was.
But another "death" I have known through it,
renewing the energy I need for striving,

and as phoenix eagle, I fly again,
with the fire a part of my feathers always.

# Háskólavísur 2014–2016

## 01: Infamous Foods

I ate today some infamous foods:
an Icelandic lunch of little delicacies.
I hail Heimdall for the hapless ram
whose soured bollocks smeared my crackers.
The fat of the whale is flavorless also,
pickled in acid ere 'twas placed on bread,
but the pungent shark powerfully lingers:
the smallest bit still smells the kitchen.

## 02: The Winds of Reykjavík

Whistling winds were whipping about,
and sideways rain had soaked my clothes.
Oft is the weather in Iceland's capital,
but to fimbul flurries, forward I look,
and the wondrous white of winter's beauty,
ere darkness deep draws o'er the land.

## 03: My Heathen Hof

"Hof" is my room: a heathen temple
to higher learning, where a horn is raised
to the elder gods of the Medieval North.
Repeating paradigms, I practice Old Norse,
and runes are written for raising consciousness.
The tales of knights by Chrétien I read,
and grails are sought for gain in my soul.
Of a Corpus of Lit, I acquire knowledge,
and mead is made for many to enjoy.

## 04: Imagine Peace Tower

On October 9, 2014, the Skald got to see the annual lighting of the Imagine Peace Tower, an outdoor work of art by Yoko Ono, located on Viðey Island just off the coast of Reykjavík in Iceland. Its name in Icelandic, Friðarsúlan (The Pillar of Peace), immediately reminded him of the ancient heathen toast, *til árs ok friðar* (for abundance and peace). From there, he wondered if perhaps a second tower was needed, a hypothetical Árssúlan ("The Pillar of Year" in Modern Icelandic, but in Old Norse, *ár* also has meanings of plenty, abundance, and fruitfulness). Thus he wrote this verse:

On fair Viðey is the Friðarsúlan,
a pillar for peace in this pleasant land.
But lacking still is a luminous tower
for abundant boons to bless the world,
Iceland's Árssúlan, for the ancients knew,
in the elder toast, "til árs ok friðar,"
that peace and plenty must prosper together.

## 05: First Snow in Reykjavík

On October 20, 2014, the first snow accumulation of the season fell on Reykjavík. Then Eirik composed this verse:

Reykjavík's snow rested on the ground,
an October morning autumnal delight.
Its fair flurries had fallen at night
on the sleeping city at sea-shore's edge.
But the winter wonder, welcomed too soon,
had melted down in muddled drizzle,
with a likeness of memory left in waters
that the well of wyrd had away taken.

# 06: The Battles of Sæmundargata

The onslaught of work spewed forth by the semester grew greater and greater, and it seemed to Eirik that attempts to get ahead of it were succeeding less than they had before. But the semester was mortally wounded, and the brave Skald knew that he had only to fight a little bit longer. On December 12, 2014, final victory was gained. The Skald had conquered, and the semester lay dead at last. Then Eirik composed this verse:

Black Knight's challenge at bridge was first.
Though "none shall pass," a knowledge contest,
a test of essays, on Chrétien's romances,
was faced in battle and defeated it lay.
Old Icelandic, the other exam,
with proud paradigms was proffered next:
translations galore were laid in ink;
I braved this exam with bloody wound,
when the slippery ice had sought its due.
The final battle was Friday morning
—many then marched to meet their wyrd—
with rising sun o'er Reykjavík,
at last laid low was the Lit-Corpus!
O'er beers and burgers, the brave rejoiced.

# 07: Nýtt Ár Ríma

Having reached at last the end of 2014, the skald and his lady enjoyed two Icelandic New Year's traditions—the bonfires and fireworks. Then Eirik composed this *ríma* in the *ferskeytt* meter:

Mighty bonfire, burning fierce,
brightly will shine, searing.
Deep it will the darkness pierce,
undimmed things appearing.

Glögg, cookies, and carefree talk
carry an hour timely;
pass this eve, with partner walk,
prowl the town sublimely.

Flying quickly, fireworks bright
fill the dark that's cloudy.
Chipper crowd on cheerful night
is chill and not rowdy.

# 08: Climb the Mountain

On a fine February day in Iceland, the intrepid students of Viking Studies walked the lands once tread by Njáll, Gunnar, and others from *Njáls saga*, and climbed the steep hill known as Stóri-Dímon near Hlíðarendi. Eirik skald was with them. The Skald reflected on spiritual pursuits, the metaphor of the climb, and the magnificence of the view from the top compared to the bottom. Then he composed this verse:

Clear cold crisp air: it cuts sharply,
but victory's view from 'vantaged point
above the abyss is the best of sights.
Below on land, we lumber around,
walking sleepers, wet and humid,
but few are those who face within
and turn their thoughts to tackling the heights.
The bold brave souls embrace the challenge
to climb the mountain, becoming dry,
and join the gods in the glorious sky.

## 09: The Heart of the Slain

The spring semester had attacked with a greater force than the fall semester, but Eirik skald had read the runes aright and was even more prepared this time around. In late March, the semester's elite vanguard, a particular long essay, had fallen like Hrungnir, leaving the rest of its forces utterly demoralized. The Skald proceeded to easily strike down the rest one by one, until the semester had only two champions remaining, at which point the Skald celebrated a brief rest with rum and cigars. As the Skald prepared to face those last two champions, he reflected on the most Sacred Heart that he had won from the slain essay and composed this verse:

I sought the Grail, that sacred Stone,
in tales time-tested of the Trú Norræn
and found my goal in those famed kernels,
the Sacred Heart of the slain Högni,
which trembled not, though taken from him,
and the steadiest stone of a stalwart ettin,
one brave enough to battle Thor
in bold combat on the border land:
Hrungnis Hjarta, hardened and spiked.
Through essay I carved this awesome gain,
attested in glyphs on the treasures of Gotland,
in mind and memory for my might's increase:
the Holy Valknut, the Heart of the Slain.

# 10: The Suns of Summer

The days passed and lengthened as the spring semester came to its final end, with the Skald having won total victory over all the classes and exams. But it was time to head onward to future adventures. After a tearful goodbye, the Skald left Iceland, returning to his homeland just in time for the hot and humid summer and its bright and searing sun. After a long rest, the Skald reflected on his travels, the sun as a metaphor, and his upcoming journey to Norway and composed this verse:

In sorrow I left for southern lands,
alone to fly and from my lady parted,
to a sleep of a sort in a summer rest.
It readies my heart for the road ahead,
for new opportunities and needful adventures.
The suns of summer, searing brightly,
give guidance and grace for the goals I seek
through healing heat and harsh strong light:
both outer sun and inner sun,
the bright day sun and black dark sun.
They rise and set and right my heading
as I turn my thoughts to the travels ahead
in that elder land of the old Bragi
for seeking the Runes and seeking the Mead.

# 11: Nýtt Land og Nýja Hof

As the summer heat of his homeland approached its peak, the Skald prepared his ship to sail from Vinland onward to new adventures in Norway. Aided by runes of good fortune, the sailing was smooth, and the Skald beached his ship in the bay and established his farmstead of Nýja Hof in the cozy little village of Sogn Studentby in the northern part of Oslo. Unlike the somewhat barren landscape of Reykjavík, this place was teeming with grass and trees, and the sun was still bright and warm. Once settled in and ready for the start of classes, the Skald noted that it was the day of a new moon, reflected on the seasonal cycles and the work ahead (especially that of his master's thesis), and composed this verse:

A bright sun shines on my bold adventure,
which now continues in a new country.
In Bragi's land, I've beached my ship
and settled in for seeking my goals
of runes and poetry through rites of study.
This heathen's New Hof is hallowed for work
that's life-changing o'er the long winter.
Through thoughts and words, my thesis work
will grow from acorn to glorious oak
in nine of moons in this northern land,
and I'll sail next summer with a self remade
for further adventures in the future's ocean.

## 12: The Semester Sets In

As the equinox passed and night began to overtake day in the ancient Viking land of Oslo, the Skald was well settled into his studies for the fall semester, which included ancient runes, the rhetoric of the elder skalds, and the tongue and poetry of the noble Anglo-Saxons. (Just like the last two semesters, he couldn't resist signing up for four classes this time around.) Never content to leave anything to the last minute, the Skald's thoughts also turned to the future and where he might next live the life of the mind, although that was still a long way off. Looking further forward to the winter break and writing a thesis in the next semester, he then composed this verse:

Dark drains daylight as I dare the Ascent:
for forty credits I further go,
as summer fades and fall comes soon.
Runes and Rhetoric rule this season
with the Anglo-Saxons' elder language;
ahead I look to a higher degree,
to set the city that I'll sail to next.
Cold December will bring courses' ends,
daytime darkness, the drifting snows,
and a final rest that's right before
the thunderous peak of thesis work.

# 13: The Turning Wheel

Autumn rolled on as the months passed. The Skald finished his first semester courses in time to celebrate his birthday in a state of total rest. December was not so cold in Oslo as one might have expected. January made up for it, however, when winter arrived in earnest. After that birthday rest, however, a protracted fight with doctoral program applications commenced. It dragged on longer than expected, running into mid-January, but at last it was finished. The new year brought a new semester, the last of the Skald's MA/MPhil in Viking and Medieval Norse Studies, which held some long-awaited treats: his master's thesis and an advanced runology course, the latter to be examined by trial lecture. Once in the thick of things, the Skald considered his situation, and composed this verse:

The turning wheel brought time for rest,
as I completed courses and passed the solstice.
The future is foggy for my further studies,
but at last the apps are left behind,
clearing my mind for the current work.
The final stretch I face this spring,
as the climbing sun calls to my soul,
as the longer light is lifting me up.
I honor Óðinn for the ale of inspiration
and call to Bragi for a builder's craft
in working words with wode and eloquence
for a thought-filled thesis, thick with the ferment
of a strong-strain yeast from my studious years,

and the final treat of a trial lecture
on the elder and younger of the ancient runes.

# 14: The End of the Degree

The cold Oslo winter persisted, and the Skald fortified himself for the long siege, working diligently on his master's thesis. But after 15 weeks, as winter's assault finally relented, the Skald finished his glorious text of 36,000 words about his ancient counterpart, the figure of the skald as found in the probable works of Snorri Sturluson: *Edda*, *Heimskringla*, and *Egils saga*. After a brief celebration and much relaxing that included plenty of sightseeing, the Skald prepared to face the final contest in his master's degree. With his lady from his time in Iceland by his side once more, he undertook the ordeal of a trial-by-lecture in a runology course and emerged victorious. It is said he celebrated the day with fine rum and a cigar in the afternoon, and by a sushi dinner and a bottle of mead with his lady in the evening. He rested the next day, composing this verse:

My wode had waxed through the winter's dark
and opened my flow of artful words.
O'er pages of ink, I poured the Mead,
revealing the tales of valiant skalds
who lived and recited their lines to kings
in the ancient north. I ordered the work
with careful skill and accord to the skalds,
rightly arranged. The runes were last,
and in warmer weather my wisdom was shown
with a trial-by-lecture to test my knowledge
of these mighty mysteries. For the Master of Arts,
my work is accomplished. I've won the victory,

a noble triumph, for truly now
this Skald has done great scholarly deeds!

# 15: Saga's End

With the work of his MA/MPhil finished, it was left to the Skald to relax and enjoy early summer and the outdoor life in Oslo with his lady. Many hills, forests, lakes, sea shores, and islands were explored. But his time to leave Europe finally arrived, and after another tearful goodbye, the Skald finally departed Oslo to visit Iceland once more on his way home to Vinland. There, the Skald rejoiced in seeing many happy and familiar sights once more, such as Háskóli Íslands, Gullfoss, Geysir, Þingvellir (including the Ásatruarfélagið's midsummer Þingblót), and Bláa Lónið. Finally, the Skald attended his graduation on June 25. After nearly eleven months abroad, the Skald returned to Vinland on June 30. Though his future directions were as yet uncertain, it was a time to celebrate further and enjoy the company of family and friends. With his time in the Viking and Medieval Norse Studies program finally finished, the Skald composed this verse:

Sweet celebrations sealed my triumph,
a victory won in Viking Studies.
Then Norway's nature was a needed break:
from my work indoors and my work within,
outer beauty to balance the inner.
On excellent Iceland, my eyes once more
were set for a time as I saw again
that lovely land. Delightful walks
—great scenic views and my graduation—
refreshed my spirit. Finally now,
at saga's end, I've sailed back home

with gainful degrees, great memories,
and a self transformed, soaring to new heights.
The sacred lights, both solar and polar,
are brightly shining on my boundless future.


The Skald's adventures will continue, but here ends *Eiríks saga Háskólavísna*.

# Invocations

## Xicoy Invocation

Xicoy, Xicoy, O chocolate goddess,
come forth from temples and forests of rain!
Open my heart with your holy power,
expanding its space for Spirit's entry.
Let's play together as partners now
on a joyful journey, O gentle Heart Blood!

## Theobroma Invocation

Food of the gods, fain I eat you!
O Theobroma, brighten my thoughts!
O Ásafœði, enable my spirit!
This is thy flesh, and thou art a god:
grant me thy grace, to godhood raise me,
as you fill and inform my fullest Self!

## Cigar Invocation

O boon-filled cigar, grant your blessings
to me in communion with the mighty spirits
of your fine tobaccos through their fiery combustion!
I've clipped your cap to cut an opening
for the inspiring flow of your special essence;
I bring fire to your foot to effect our rite
and with breath draw forth your blazing main!
Let your wispy white clouds bring welcome joy
and exalt my thoughts with etheric energy.
May your fragrant smoke refill my soul!

## Cigarillo Invocation

O sweet cigarillo, small but mighty,
I light your foot; now lift my spirits
as we commune in these welcome moments
of pleasure and joy, peacefully together.

## Cannabis Invocation

O great green lion, glorious cannabis,
I partake of your essence through powerful smoke;
give to my soul the solar gold
that your maw consumed, sanctified with main.
Open the gates to the upper realms,
exalting my senses to a zenith of clarity.

# Hrapé Invocation

Hail Mapacho, O potent Master,
and the herbs and ashes that are all blended
in this sacred hrapé. I seek Spirit:
open my way to the upper world,
with eagle wings I aim for Ascent.
I call for your craft to cleanse and empower.
I attend to your teachings for truth and wisdom.
I hark to your help for healing and love.

## Coffee Invocation

O craft-filled coffee, with a cup I invoke
your blessed bean juice for brightest wakefulness
as a dreamer of the day for my deeds of might.
O dispeller of sleep, my spirit takes flight
with the rising aroma of your roasted grounds
as your dark hot drink now drives my works.
O jitter java, the jolt you bring
is a welcome buzz that waxes my speed
as now I drink of your noble boons!

## Water Invocation

O water so holy,
wellspring of life,
grant me your brightest blessings
of health, vigor,
happiness, victory,
and wynful might and main.

# Call to the Green Fairy

O Green Fairy,
glorious lady,
I call on thee to come!
Angel of awe,
in absinthe thou dwellest,
and now thy draught I drink.

To thy wormwood wine,
some water I added,
to release thy louche of herbs.
Sucrose sweet
I set on the spoon
to feed and fuel thy spirit.

Rightful ritual
readied thy gift,
changed from clear to cloudy,
and soon my soul
will soar in heights,
changed from cloudy to clear.

O mighty muse,
my mind is ready:
my ghost I give to thee!
Fly forth now,
O Fairy of Green:
come and clasp me here,
come and wax my wode!

# Moldavite Invocation

Hail Moldavite, O mighty Stone,
both Fire and Earth in a fusion that's Dry,
verily linked to vital Gold:
give me alchemist gnosis in the Art of Self.
O Vital Vltavín, thou art a verdant Grail;
spur my Ascent with thy Solar Spirit,
give me polar puissance as a piece of aurora.
O star-born stone, make stellar my heart!

# Solar Glory Invocation

O Sol Invicte, may thy sacred light
be shining in my holy Heart,
and with Mithras' might, mantle my spirit
in the dignity of a kingly cloak,
as I raise my scepter of sovereign rule
and reach the realm of the gods,
by seeking thy gold for solar glory
and a regal rank through Ascent.

## Runic Sun Invocation

O Sun of Runes, assign me your boons:
the power to rise o'er opponents' lies,
the eternal Fire of your twirling gyre,
and a Center inside of Solar pride.

# Round Table Sun Wheel Invocation

O Round Table, O Rune Sun Wheel
with the Holy Grail as your glorious hub,
I seek Ascent on your Solar path
as a worthy Knight of the wondrous Quest.
Grant me your boons: to grow in Spirit,
to serve the King, to carry Tradition,
to defend the Center, to feel Compassion,
to ask the Question, to ken the Fire,
and to strive always for the stellar Ideal.

www.ingramcontent.com/pod-product-compliance
Lightning Source LLC
Chambersburg PA
CBHW060529080526
44586CB00012B/674